BRAND YOU
LIKE A BOSS

A No Fluff Guide on Building A
Personal Brand People Know,
LOVE & Trust

NATASHA WESTON

BRAND YOU LIKE A BOSS

For information contact:

NatashaWeston.com

BrandYouLikeABoss.com

Library of Congress Control Number: 2017906077

ISBN: 978-0983218777

ISBN-10: 0983218773

Book and Cover design by Jasmine Easter

Author Photography by Jake Simpson

Published by Grace Us Living Publications

CONTENTS

"Nobody built like you, you designed yourself."

Jay 3

INTRODUCTION

BRANDING. BRANDING. BRANDING. Ladies and gentlemen, I introduce to you the #1 buzz word of the century! Let me guess, you picked up this book because you are curious to know what all the branding hype is about. Maybe you are an entrepreneur that has read tons of books on the subject, but still can't wrap your brain around what it means. Perhaps you are sitting on your 9-5 wondering how to snag the position that just opened in your department. Whatever reason you decided to open this read, I am glad you are here.

Personal branding has never been more popular than it is now...EVER! We have always heard of the bigger brands like Apple, which was birthed from Steve Job's genius; The OWN Network, which stemmed from Oprah's natural ability to make people feel good; The Obama Legacy, which will forever be remembered from the warmth of Michelle and Barak's touchable persona, during their time in the White House; and even President Donald Trump. Some are not big fans, but if you look back at his history, he too had a personal brand, even before he became the 45th President of the United States of America. He probably had more fans in his Apprentice days, but his personal brand did what every personal brand on this planet should do. It should make you either love it or hate it.

Since writing my first book, I had a reality check. A serious one! I literally shut down my first business, and was forced to look myself in the mirror. I had to figure out exactly what was, and was not working in my business. My desire was to build an organic and loyal community of people, who would not only buy what I had to offer, but would grow as I evolved. I later found my solution, by refocusing from building a business, to tapping into my personal brand. Yes, I had a business, but who doesn't? What I lacked was a genuine connection. A connection that would not only allow my business to soar, but would allow me to be me, and be completely unapologetic.

One of the biggest lessons I have learned that has cost me lots of time, energy and money is, if you build the "brand of you" first, you can sell anything. As I think back, personal branding was not something I understood, focused on or acknowledged for a very long time. Truth is, I was just like many of you. A part of me knew I was born to lead, but did not know much more than that. I wanted to have a great impact in changing my life, and the lives of others. I had what seemed to be a weird obsession with making that impact. It "looked good." I wanted what every other person at one point or another wanted, the lights, camera, action. From the outside looking in, I had the perfect brand, but the truth was, I had no idea what was going on. I had been featured on blogs, in magazines, on television and radio, but I was still broke and struggling financially. Honestly, I did not tap into the power of my very own personal brand until years later. I had a business that was familiar to many, but that was not enough. It seems I could not attract the right people into my world, but couldn't figure out why. I knew I had to change some things, starting with myself. Self-evaluation has and will be one of the most challenging things we will ever do in this lifetime. However, this is the most critical step in discovering your personal brand.

My intent in this book is not to get too deep and personal. However, my main mission is to address many of the questions I receive daily. It's funny how life works. In my years as an entrepreneur, I had no idea just how many people were witnessing the incredible growth of my brand. Heck, I did not know I had one, or any idea why it was important for my life's development. It is a continual growing process, and I am growing into the person that I want to be. I now have a clearer direction on where I want to go personally and professionally. As I look back on many of the experiences encountered, I realize it was all molding and shaping my blueprint.

Fast forward to now, we are here! Personal branding is a hot topic everywhere. From blogs to social media, live events and books, personal branding is probably one of the most talked about topics on the planet. It has so much freedom! More people are becoming aware of the possibilities of creating the life you desire, around who you are authentically.

Long gone the days where you must be a singer, athlete or political figure to have influence, or the power to change your lifestyle. We now live in an era where you can literally create a movement on social media, and get tons of fans to connect with you. It is possible, within a matter of time be "seen as" an authority or leader in your field. This is no exaggeration either. We have seen people, from all walks of life, Kim Kardashian to K. Michelle, literally transform their personal brands into businesses. The world is infatuated!

Many familiar personal brands of our time were birthed the untraditional way. It has been proven that it is possible to be whoever you want to be in this lifetime. The moment I realized I had this same potential, all barriers were broken. I could no longer be contained with ideas, thoughts and the opinions of others that said I had to live a traditional life to become successful. In fact, at this very moment, I am giving you permission to break those same barriers that are holding your shine hostage.

I had intensely studied just about every popular book on personal growth and development, branding and followed some of the most interesting personal brands known in our time. I still could not grasp the true essence of how to tap into the real Natasha, without seeming to exhibit a self-indulging and "all about me" attitude.

The main reason I wanted to write this book was because I can honestly say, I have finally figured out how to build a personal brand. Another great thing is, you don't have to be an entrepreneur or business owner to have one. Looking back at my life prior to having a business, every experience was a piece of the puzzle. I could not shy away from this fact. It is important to learn to embrace where you came from, where you are, and learn to leverage those experiences. This is how you create your own blueprint around every aspect of your life. Your brand is created from your lifestyle, political views, opinions and the not so great "situations". As a result, you will create a strong brand presence that will reap many benefits.

This journey includes, how you identify the problems that provide solutions to those who are attracted to your personal brand. When you can create the solutions to people's need and desires, this is how you build the know, like and trust factors. As a result, you become the expert, and your reputation and personal brand grows. One of my biggest goals when I started acknowledging the power of my personal brand, was to become well known for solving problems. While I continued to build, the everyday harsh challenges in life did not cease. I had to live through and deal with the problems and issues I struggled with on a daily basis. In the beginning, ninety percent of my personal brand was built from a negative balanced bank account, failed relationships and back rent. Using the excuse that money has stopped you from getting intentional, and building the brand of your dreams is not a good excuse. Therefore, you can kick that excuse to the curb. Been there done that!

Back to my point. I wanted people to identify me for the problems I solved, that many people never overcome. One example is starting a business while working a day job with no startup funds. I wrote a book about it. Once upon a time this was a problem area for me, but I figured out how to make it work. Essentially, I created something based off a problem, discovering that others were having the exact same challenges. I simply provided a solution by communicating my story in the form of a book. That one challenge, has now positioned me as an expert. This resulted in being invited to travel the country, speak to entrepreneurs, and share my life.

I am creating a life around who I am authentically. It is not a made-up story or a social media fairytale. Being transparent, makes it so much easier to connect with others. It can become easy to get caught up with people who are not being completely transparent about their lives. The best thing you can do in life and in business, is to know the value in being your true self.

I also want you to understand, it does not matter if you work in corporate America; or at the local McDonalds. There is much you can do to advance and excel in the workplace. I believe, everything we do outside of the workplace, is a contribution to who we are in the workplace. Later in this book, I will discuss how personal branding influences your performance on the job. These experiences increase your ability to provide superb customer service. Your personal brand at work, contributes to how people perceive you, and what your coworkers and supervisors say about you when you are not around. These are all factors in getting a raise or promotion.

Let's just say, you are already an entrepreneur with an existing personal brand. Maybe you have a stain on your reputation that needs fixing, or have made a career transition. If you would like to be seen as more than "the PR girl," you will need to know how to rebrand yourself. Brand You Like A Boss, will provide you with tips on how to give your brand a facelift, and how to reposition yourself to refocus (or shift) the conversation.

Despite what you may have been told, you determine what people say and think about you. I believe that ninety percent of what people think about us is based off what we embed in their minds, rather we do it on purpose or not. Keep in mind, everything that we post on social media, how we treat others and how we interact, are all ways of crafting our own brand story.

Now here's the real deal: Personal branding is not that deep. People make it more difficult than it is, not realizing that you are already building your brand. I did not want this book to be just another book of branding terms and definitions you could find on Google. This book is going to show you how to go beyond the definition. You will learn how to be your authentic self, and add strategy to create the life that you want, and build a brand that people know, LOVE and trust.

Cultivating your brand before starting a business or getting a promotion, is equally as important as taking care of your mind, body and soul.

In this book, I am sharing how I went from unintentionally crafting my own blueprint, to having a personal brand that others are raving about. This book is for entrepreneurs in real life, entrepreneurs at heart, authors, speakers, influencers, pastors, artists and anyone who desires to build an authentic and timeless personal brand.

"Be you. The world will catch up."

 #BRANDYOULIKEABOSS

I Am A Brand...Duh!

My Personal Brand Story

It was late 2011, and I hit rock bottom within the four imaginary walls of my very first business, Eloquence Enterprises. I was broke, client-less and questioning rather or not I would ever be fit to live the entrepreneur life. I started Eloquence from the day bed in my aunt's Bronx apartment. Prior to that, I was on a mission to become America's Next Top Fashion Stylist, but that too seemed to be a major fail. Truth is, I was just another entrepreneur, stuck behind a computer, hoping that someone would notice me. Desperately, I hoped my talents would be discovered, and I would make it big in New York City. Boy was I wrong!

I began this business extremely passionate. I just knew it would go far. I seemed to enjoy the surface layer of all things public relations, media and fashion.

19

Well, I got way ahead of myself. Being in that business three years, I not only lost my business, but also, the real Natasha. Somehow, I drowned in the sea of being in the business of everyone else. I had mastered learning about the who's who in my industries. What I had not mastered, was my own self and the true power that was on the inside of me.

I faced the music and officially shut down my business, on top of living back at home with my mom. This time seemed familiar. Too familiar. It felt like déjà vu. Literally! If you read my first book, I wrote about it in "10 Effective Ways to Start Your Business With 0 Dollars." Do you remember? Yep, same saga, but this time was different. Through natural eyes, I may have looked as though I had failed, but I had not.

The sequence of my own personal story had to play out so I could share it. This could not happen, stuck behind someone else or someone else's brand. It was time to take the mask off, and step into my own, for real.

I put together a plan and strategy of what to do next. It all started with YouTube videos. I had never in my life stood in the front of a camera, so as you can probably imagine, I was terrified about a few things:

1. How would I look?
2. What would people say or think about me?
3. Did I have enough of a story to share yet?
4. Would anyone care about what I had to say?

Regardless of how many fears I had, I did it anyway. During this time, I did not realize, this would be the start of what was to be my personal brand. At 25 years old, I had already gone through some incredible experiences, both good and bad. I knew, to make the impact and gain the influence I so deeply desired, I had to get in front of the camera and open my mouth. There was no other way, so I did just that. My second business was birthed, The Tottie Brand.

My original vision for The Tottie Brand was to become a world-renowned speaker and brand ambassador for major corporations. I also envisioned myself hosting events, and becoming a huge digital influencer. I had big dreams for this new business. Excited, I planned my first big photo shoot with the best photographer in the city. I created a logo, and partnered with a well-known influencer at her local fashion boutique to celebrate the launch. On June 20, 2013, I officially birthed my very own personal brand.

As I walked through the doors of Social Butterfly Boutique in Mauldin, South Carolina, I had no idea what to expect. What I did not expect was an empty house. Like my first event, Unmask the Swag in 2011, not many people showed up to celebrate my big day. Those who attended were the boutique customers, my mom, and a couple of the owner's friends. Although any effort is a success, I learned a big lesson on the day I officially launched my personal brand. **The lesson: No one knows your story! If no one knows your story, what is the point?** The story behind the brand that is.

I made the investments in the look of my brand, but I questioned what was missing? I discovered the biggest that the most important piece of the brand puzzle missing was my story. I started to evaluate and piece together all the reasons why my first business failed, and why in the phase of launching a second one, still no real success. I concluded I would have to rethink how I was going about all of this. I made one of the most common mistakes that many make: Your business and your personal brand are not the same. Was the message I exemplified cohesive with the "perfect picture" glamour shot in the yellow peplum dress that was seen in Today's Black Woman Magazine and on VibeVixen.com.

Only I could face the true facts that my personal brand was my truth and I was hiding it.

October 26, 2014: I sat down at the table in the dining room of our small two-bedroom townhouse in Greenville, SC. I recorded my first motivational video titled "Feeling Stuck." In this video, I was on a mission to motivate and encourage my peers by discussing topics I was well versed in. Feeling stuck was one experience I had encountered too many times, so I wanted to address it and be as transparent as possible. This was easier said than done. As I recorded these first videos, I lacked confidence and was still trying to figure out my own way! I did not have the perfect recording set up and recorded with my "not so smart" phone.

At that time, I had no idea I was building what I now call, my digital resume. After recording over ten videos, I became more open to discussing some of the biggest challenges and lessons of my entire life. Taking a leap and getting on camera, taught me one of the first important lessons of personal branding. Your brand starts wherever you are. This was the start of something great.

June 26, 2015: I walked in the doors of my local Barnes & Nobles Bookstore on Haywood Road in Greenville, SC. I was featured in one of the largest beauty magazines in the country, Sheen Magazine. The issue hit stands on this day. I was both nervous and excited to get such great exposure. More importantly, for the first time, I was sharing a different part of my brand story that I had not yet shared.

The magazine feature positioned me to share one of my biggest insecurities. My ability to do that, would take my brand to a whole new level of the word "transparent!" To uncover and discuss one of my biggest child hood struggles, would cause me to be seen in a different light. This story would show a new dimension of who I was. It was a very intricate part of my brand story. Though I struggled, I knew I had to share.

This is when I learned the next biggest lesson of personal branding. The not so glamourous, vulnerable or enticing experiences of your life, are the key components of what draws people emotionally to your brand.

In this half page article, I shared how I was bullied as a child because of a slight cosmetic imperfection, on the left side of my nose. Until I got to high school, I seriously struggled because I did not look like everyone else. Boys would tease and call me names. I tried everything to get rid of it, including meeting with plastic surgeons at the age of 10. As I got older, I realized it was EXACTLY that small "imperfection" that defined and made me unique. Isn't it funny when we are young, we do everything to look and be like everyone else. Now as adults, business owners and entrepreneurs, we want to do everything we can to set ourselves apart? Gosh, I am glad I decided to keep my cosmetic "imperfection" as a side kick.

This article, accompanied with a very intimate confessional video, forever changed the dynamics of my brand. For the first time, my audience did not just see the surface level. They connected with me because they could relate to an in your face, real-life experience, through this part of my story.

September 6, 2016: I hit rock bottom, and I vlogged to tell all 15,000+ social media friends about it. For sympathy? No. I wanted to take the noose from around my neck. The noose that was holding me bound to a year of nothing but pure struggle. Before posting this video on Facebook, I can remember telling my mom in the car I felt like I was suffocating. Suffocating because I was not being open and honest about what we had just gone through. I knew I could not hold it in anymore, as if it were some big secret. As the days went by, I felt more like a hypocrite. A hypocrite because for years I had been preaching the "Your circumstances don't define you" sermon. How dare I experience such a life changing event, and not share my testimony with those who had been loyal followers of my brand. I bet you are wondering what in the world could have happened that caused me to feel this way. Well, let me give it to you in a nutshell. Just 30 days prior to posting the video that changed my entire life and business; I received some not so great news.

My family and I learned, we would have to move out of the house we had just settled back into, not even a year prior. After illegally losing this same home ten years ago, I found myself in a very devastating place, questioning why God would allow this to happen again. With a drained bank account, and very little motivational support, I had to pull the motivation I had instilled inside of myself. I had to use the motivational energy within myself to push me through this painful transition. God used this transition to give me clarity and more power. More than ever before, I had to motivate the thousands of people who had been following my journey for over eight years. I realized through all this, just how much people underestimate the power of motivation. Motivation was exactly what allowed me to dominate one of the biggest storms of my entire life. Less than a month later, a new dimension of my personal brand was born...The Motivation Maven.

No, I did not need a college degree or the perfect life story to attract an audience. My REAL and raw story organically multiplied my influence. Many could relate to something that happened to me. Let's just say my personal brand has not been the same since. Finally, people started to know, LOVE and trust me.

"Your brand starts wherever you are."

 #BRANDYOULIKEABOSS

Personal Branding Basics

Now let's talk branding. This word has been tossed around and mishandled more than ever, over the last century. Whenever the topic of personal branding comes up in conversations and among new entrepreneurs, it is typically confused with marketing. Branding and marketing are forever used interchangeably. However, it is vital you understand the difference. Years later, after starting The Tottie Brand, I only had a surface level understanding of branding, like many others. I couldn't tap into the essence of what my very own personal brand stood for, until I lived it each day. Personal branding is not just something you switch on and off like a light switch. A true and authentic one is a part of who you are. Effective personal branding is not an overnight achievement. It is an ongoing process that allows and encourages you to grow, evolve and reinvent yourself, every time the opportunity presents itself. This is where most people get confused about the subject. A well-defined personal brand does three specific things:

1. **It attracts** *(through great messaging and powerful visuals)*
2. **It retains** *(through superb marketing)*
3. **It inspires** *(by showing compassion and providing extreme value to your audience)*

As someone who has studied personal branding, created my very own blueprint and have assisted clients to do the same, I have come up with a very simple definition for personal branding. Personal branding is simply where your personality and strategy collide. It is the language you speak in life. Personal branding is:

- **What you say**
- **What you do**
- **How you respond**
- **How you interact**

If you have a business, your personal brand becomes an asset when done with strategy and intention. If you work a nine to five, it becomes the differentiating factor in relationship building and corporate elevation.

Before we move on, let me introduce you to The BIG Question. The BIG Question is simply asking yourself what do you want to be known for. What do you want people to say about you when you are not around? Let's try it together, fill in the blank: "I want to be known for/as_____.

This is where you set the tone and predict the future of your personal brand. All you do is start from the inside out and craft your brand by filling in the blanks. The blanks consist of:

- **Who you are?**
- **What you stand for?**
- **What your values are?**

- **What should people know about you?**

The next level of personal branding is all about being intentional. This is where the strategy comes in. Great strategies will allow you to map out a plan to answer The BIG Question. I hope that you are following the map here.

In the same way branding and marketing are often confused, so is what branding is not. Branding is not just a logo, trademark or your website. These are called your brand elements. They are important, but only after you have dug in the core, identified your brand story and filled in the blanks. Building and crafting a strong and authentic personal brand is a great way to build the know, love and trust in your business or in the workplace. It adds extreme value to your audience, and to everyone you interact with on your job.

A WELL-DEFINED PERSONAL BRAND:
- ATTRACTS
- RETAINS
- INSPIRES

#BRANDYOULIKEABOSS

It's simple. When people are attracted to you, the brand, they will likely invest in your business, ideas and goals. When your coworkers and the leaders in your company feel a part of your brand story, they are more likely to be invested in your career growth. STOP! Before you flip another page, here is the raw truth: Nothing in this book will work for you, if you lack the ability to be consistent.

Consistency is the name of the game, and you must be willing to show up (*singing) "through the good, bad, happy or sad." Talk about the immediate memory of Barack Obama singing that tune on national television. We will never forget it. Now, that my friend is how you show up! Ok, let's get back to the subject at hand...consistency.

Whenever I meet a new client, or someone hits me up in my Facebook DMs about building their personal brands, one of the first questions I ask is, "What have you been doing up until now to build it?" This is a very important question. Again, personal branding is not that deep. Some people make it appear to be that deep because we fail to be consistent in our endeavors.

A major part of a strong and effective personal brand is visibility. The very least you can do to build your brand is to simply show up. Showing up is the foundation you need to attract others to the brand of you. If you do not show up, why should they? Although uncomfortable at times, stepping beyond your boundaries and considering the impact that showing up and sharing your unique story is key. Your story's value is vital to the success of your personal brand plan.

I hope by now, you get the just of the technical meaning of personal branding. Let's wrap this up. In a nutshell, your personal brand answers the question of what are people are saying about you when you are not in the room.

Whatever they are saying is determined by the look, messaging and network that you are associated with. I now introduce to you, The LMN Approach™.

PART ONE

The LMN Approach™

As a brand strategist, one of the top statements I hear constantly is "I want to build my personal brand, but I don't know where to begin." I know this task can sound daunting, however, personal branding is quite simple if you use a 3-part framework. I coined this framework to make sure I did not leave out the most important elements of my personal brand over the years.

After working one-on-one with dozens of clients, I took note of the processes and systems I was using. Noticing patterns in the startup and cultivation of their personal brands, three things were consistently being considered. No matter who they were and what industry they were a part of, the following components were being considered:

1. **The Look**
2. **The Message**
3. **The Network**

All three of these areas are the makeup of an attractively strong personal brand. Your look is the first point of contact between you and your audience. Your messaging is your brand story. Your network is your visibility and ability to properly position yourself in the front of those who you wish to share your message and unique value with.

Before we dive into the specifics of the LMN framework, I want you to know that these three parts do not necessarily have to go in order. However, notice they do fall in the order in which our audiences interact with us. First, they are judging you by how you and your brand looks with the physical eye. Think about the last person you went to find on Instagram. You glanced at their avatar and the first few pictures on their timeline. This is THE LOOK of the LMN Approach™.

Second, if their avatar and timeline photos were attractive, you probably clicked on one of those photos to read the caption. You then connected with that person's message. This person could be the CEO of your favorite clothing company or a single mommy blogger, but you connected with their story. This is THE MESSAGE of The LMN Approach™.

Lastly, if you connected with that person's messaging, you probably went on and hit the follow button. Why? You wanted more! You wanted to know what else this personal brand could offer you. Can you guess what you did next? Well, you clicked on the infamous "link in bio" and probably opened your wallet after that. You are now a part of that person's network. You will buy into what they are serving and if it tastes good, you will share them with someone else. This is THE NETWORK of The LMN Approach™.

This exact framework has become the canvas in which I have built my own personal brand. It is the guide I introduce to each client who hires me to help them "build a personal brand." The LMN Approach™ simplifies the overconsumption of the "who, what and how'", we often consider on the quest to becoming influential. As we dig deeper into each part of this framework, think of it as an empty puzzle. The framework is ready for you to fill in the pieces.

"Great photos tell the story & paint the picture of your brand."

#BRANDYOULIKEABOSS

CHAPTER ONE

Your Look

When was the last time you judged a book by its cover? Take a moment and think about it. I will wait. You know you are on the right track if you did not have to think that far back! Why? Could you have judged THIS book by its cover?

Maybe you made the decision to purchase a copy after seeing the cover shared across social media. Could you have stumbled across one of my latest photoshoot pics, or witnessed my big transformation to blonde earlier this year? Perhaps you met me at an event and loved my taste in wardrobe selection. Whatever reason, you judged me based off what you saw with your physical eye. I promise, I am not judging you. We all do it.

Many of our purchasing decisions and life choices, are made after our first interaction with something we saw. This is the first pillar of The LMN Approach™. Do not be fooled, you are being judged. As you build your brand, it is important you take into consideration every visual aspect of who you are. This can include your hair, the ensemble selected for the Chamber of Commerce event, or the graphics shared on your Instagram page. As vain as it may sound, your next opportunity could be resting upon your look.

Just think about this for a moment. Remember the rise of the "Instagram Boutique?" Well, this is the perfect example. Before everyone and their mama had an online fashion store, many of us bought our hottest pieces of clothing from the likes of Asos, Lulus and H&M. When online boutiques, like Fashion Nova surfaced, we were quickly converted into fans and customers. Why? The brand's photos on their Instagram timeline. It did not take long before other online stores popped up with no credibility and crappy images to showcase their product. What did we do? Well nothing! Our first point of contact with these no named brands were not the best experience visually. The same rules apply here. Your appearance, (both on and offline) can determine if you are presented with that next big opportunity.

Similarly, how you show up to a job interview determines if you land that dream job. You see, rather you like it or not, investing in "the look" is a major key when building your brand. Now you may be wondering where to start. I would like to break "the look", down into a few different categories:

1. **Photos**
2. **Dress/Grooming/Beauty**
3. **Visuals/Graphics**

Whenever, I score a new personal branding client, one of the first questions I ask is "Do you have any recent photos that best represent your brand personality and message?" Nine times out of ten, they do not so I quickly advise them to schedule a photo session. While you are crafting the best strategy and getting the back end of your brand set up, do not miss the opportunity to grasp the attention of a prospective customer or client. Do not get "caught slipping" using a selfie as your profile pic.

Photos

Great photos will take you far. You will get tons of usage from having professionally taken, high resolution photographs. Great photos tell the story and paint the picture of your brand. I do not think we can deny, as humans we are just visual creatures. Therefore, whenever someone is referred or we meet someone we have never met before, the first thing many of us do, is look that person up and start looking at their pictures. Hence the reason, Instagram is one of the leading social platforms to date. We want to see what people look like, what they are doing and where they are. You name it, we want to see it.

Next, I would like to share different types of photos used to help make the best first impression possible. The most popular type of photograph is the headshot. Headshots are the face behind your brand. It is a simple representation of the brain behind the business. It is the person sitting behind the desk at your organization. People want to put a face with a name, and headshots will make this possible. When I think of headshots, I cannot help but think about blind dating.

Before you go there, no I have never been on one! I can only imagine, after speaking to someone for months on the phone, you cannot wait to put a face to that person's name, conversation and actions. Ok, now let's get a little more specific. Your headshots should be taken by a professional photographer. This is to ensure you are getting the highest quality possible. When deciding on a photographer, I recommend checking out their portfolio. You want to make sure they are using the right equipment, lighting and can provide high resolution images.

Let me pause for a minute and elaborate on the importance of having high resolution photos. This quality of photograph is vital when it is time to enlarge your headshots for posters, ads or even a billboard, if that is your goal. Failure to have high resolution photos will result in a blurry and unprofessional look; that won't be a good look for your brand. Most headshots are taken in a studio. It could be on a plain, solid colored backdrop or with props, such as couches, kitchen step ups, etc. Your headshots should be current and up to date. As you grow your brand and start to expand your network, you will want your photos to be a current resemblance of you. For example, all my life I had long black hair. When I made the major transformation to blonde earlier this year, I had to take new photos to resemble how I looked in real life. Thankfully, my annual photoshoot was approaching! You will use headshots for many different things from your social media avatar to your LinkedIn profile, to press mentions on blogs or magazines.

The next type of photograph used in branding are known as lifestyle photos. These are more personality and action styled photography. They will evoke some type of emotion. When someone looks at your photo ask yourself, will they smile, get excited, inspired, or will they feel sad and want to cry? Lifestyle photos showcase your brand personality. Is your brand personality comedic, high energy or calm and inviting? These photos also provide a still image of you in action (i.e.: behind the scenes or of you out and about). These style photos are common for bloggers and influencers. For instance, think of the last Steve Harvey photo you saw. Did you laugh or feel sad? I am pretty sure you laughed! I am laughing as I type this sentence, because this is Steve's brand personality. It is often showcased in his photos.

Although you should aim to have all your photos in the highest resolution possible, lifestyle photos are typically only shared on social platforms like Instagram. In this case, seek a local lifestyle photographer who can meet with you once or twice a month, to snap some lifestyle photos for you. You can spread them throughout your content for the next month or so.

I met my lifestyle photographer Taylor on Instagram, by searching a local hashtag for photographers in my area. This is a great way to scout out the best photographers locally. The third type of photograph you may use are styled photos. These are commonly known as product photos and/or flatlays. If your personal brand is monetized through an online store, where you may sell merchandise or digital products, you can showcase those through styled photography. Styled photography is becoming more and more popular as it showcases your product in a real-life environment. Ironically, there are photographers who have niched their businesses specifically for styled stock photos. If you wanted to purchase a cool coffee mug, nine times out of ten, you will purchase from the brand that uses styled photos to showcase their coffee mug, versus a brand that simply just shares a plain photo of the mug. This is a great way to set your brand apart from other brands.

YOUR LOOK CONSISTS OF:
-PHOTOS
-DRESS/GROOMING/BEAUTY
-VISUALS/GRAPHICS

Dress/Grooming/Beauty

The next category of your look is dress and grooming. Before we begin, I would have you to know that I am at my happiest when I am makeup free and lounging around in my pink zebra Snuggie. However, when you are out in the world, being well groomed and looking your best is important. I pride myself in making sure when I step out, rather it be to speak at an event, hop on Facebook Live or during a girls night out; I always try to make sure that what I am wearing is an accurate presentation of who I am. Believe it or not, I meet a lot of potential clients and customers when I am out doing "non-work" activities! You just never know who you are going to run into. You want to be sure that how you look is a good representation of your brand.

As you grow and evolve, so will your brand. Your story will rarely change, however your look will. You want to showcase that always. I can remember planning my last branding photo shoot. I had just changed my hair color and never felt more confident in my life. I was over trying to portray myself as some sort of saint. I wanted people to still take me serious as a business woman, but I wanted them to also know that I embraced my "sexy". I enjoyed showing some skin occasionally, but in a tasteful way of course! Outside of your dress, making sure that you pay attention to things such as your breath and hygiene is also important.

Visuals/Graphics

Typically, when we think about visuals and graphics for our brands, we think website, logo, business cards, marketing materials, flyers and graphics used on social media. The goal is to make sure whatever you do, they are cohesive and visually appealing both on and offline. Considering the style or types of visuals to incorporate into your personal brand is extremely important. I am excessively passionate in this area, therefore I will try to refrain from turning this part of the book into a rant! However, I will simply point out the main factors you should consider when creating or hiring out visual/graphic elements for your branding.

The very first thing the human eye zooms in on, when interacting with the visual aspect of your personal brand are colors. What many do not know, is that all pinks are not the same and all greens are not either. You probably won't notice this if you have never been in the graphic design world. When you are hiring someone to design your logo or website, you will want to make sure they provide you with the exact color codes used. This will ensure that your colors are the exact same across the board.

Color codes are best known as HTML color codes. They represent various color families. This code is a combination of 6 letters and numbers, lead with a pound symbol (#). For example, the color code for black is #000000 and the code for white is #FFFFFF. Depending on your specific brand colors, these numbers and letters will vary. As you specify your brand color scheme, you will also want to have handy the other sub categories of a color code available like RGB and CMYK. This is important because while many graphic design platforms (Photoshop & Canva) may only require the HTML color code, word processors like Microsoft Word will only be able to use the RGB versions of your color code. You can find details about your specific color codes by simply typing your code in a Google search or by visiting www.color-hex.com. I know this may sound super techy, however it is important to know this key information so that you stick with the exact same colors both on and offline.

Another important aspect of visuals you may want to consider for consistency, are your fonts or what is commonly referred to as typography. In a nutshell, you do not want to use too many fonts in your branding. It is just not pleasant on the eye. It will give off a sense of unclarity and confusion to your audience.

My recommendation to avoid inconsistent visuals and graphics, is to invest in a brand style guide. A brand style guide is the visual DNA makeup of your brand. It is the visual Bible for every visual you create throughout your brand journey. This guide defines, describes and provides examples of what your personal brand should look like online, social media and in print media, just to name a few. There are tons of information out there on brand style guides. I highly suggest getting one so that you can be very clear on how your brand should be visually presented. Brand Style Guides are used within almost every big brand you have ever used, such as Walmart, Starbucks, Amazon and FedEx. This guide will include:

- **Your logo specifics**
- **Your brand color scheme & codes**
- **Your brand fonts/typography**
- **Your brand patterns and shapes**

Having consistent and high-quality visuals for your personal brand is going to continue to show the investment in your branding efforts. As a result, you will attract the right people.

"Your message is the core of your personal brand."

 #BRANDYOULIKEABOSS

CHAPTER TWO

Your Message

Your message is the core and it factor of your personal brand. The strength of my brand stems solely off the fact that it was built when I had absolutely nothing. Literally nothing. The only thing I had to leverage was myself, and the stories I was so afraid to reveal. Your stories are merely thoroughbred messages meant to resonate with someone else's mind, body, soul or spirit. It does not matter who you are or what that message is, your ability to communicate it through your personal brand is important.

I often hear people say they do not know how to be open and transparent about their lives. I will be the first to say, this is not an easy thing to do. To share the sometimes embarrassing, painful or less exciting parts of your life is like getting your teeth pulled out. You may not know how that feels literally, but just the thought of it probably makes you cringe. In the beginning, being transparent was my biggest struggle. Once I took the plug out, I will never forget how it transformed not only my personal brand, but my business. I did not have anything to hide and nobody could tell me anything about my life that I had not already exposed. Talk about beating the devil at his own game, haha!

The point is, I had to retrain my mind to see the positives in being open and transparent with complete strangers. I considered, what if my mentors, or the most influential people in my life stopped being transparent. What if they were to keep their most life changing experiences to themselves and not share them? How would it make me feel? Well, it would make me feel as if they were shutting me out and not letting me in. I would feel like they no longer cared that they were pulling my life line of motivation and inspiration. I would feel like the avenues in which I received information from them would be gone. When I started to reframe my mind to think about the consequences of not being transparent, I started to reap the benefits of my brand message.

The following examples are different categories of how personal brand messaging influences the different aspects of our lives.

Mind: Teachers, Coaches
Body: Physical trainers, Doctors
Soul/Spirit: Ministers, Pastors/Priests

When I say personal branding is not that deep, I mean just that. When you think of your brand, your thoughts immediately race to having the perfect story and message. Here is a reality check: Perfect stories do not change the world, messed up and real ones do. The sooner you realize this, the better.

When crafting your brand message, you want to take the aspects of your life and pull out every experience where you:

1. **Learned a valuable lesson**
2. **Solved a problem**
3. **Discovered a solution that could become a solution for someone else.**

Your goal is to take these experiences and communicate the lessons and solutions in a way that your audience and colleagues will understand. Let's say you are a young college girl who discovered that you could make money buying dated designer gear, and could flip it on eBay for more money. This would be your solution to having some pocket money to fund your shopping habits while in school. You decide to turn this "discovery" into a business, and show other young college girls how to do the same. Would you advertise your new business in the local newspaper? Nah, probably not. You are going to go and tell your discovery story exactly where almost every other young "twenty something" college girl is hanging out...on social media. If you wanted to get even more specific, you would go on Instagram and Snapchat. This would become the avenue in which your message is effectively positioned and delivered. Once you have positioned your message, you will want to create experiences by creating tangible content.

Content can literally come in many ways. If you are a pastor, your content simply will come through revelations you receive from God. If you are a motivational speaker, your content is inspired by the day to day experiences in your life. If you are a single parent, your content comes from the daily challenges you have, and the solutions that you have found in those experiences. If you are a blogger, your content comes from the things that interest you the most, such as food, travel or fashion.

The key to your personal brand messaging is to talk about the things you are passionate about. When you begin to talk about these things, naturally people who can benefit from them will start to express their. Once this happens, the trust is being built. They will then feel open enough to share their problems.

You must have a voice. Do not be the person who goes whichever way the wind blows. The most powerful brand messages are those with a voice. The ones that stand for something. If you have a firm stance on an issue, topic or idea, you become an advocate and responsible for standing for what you believe. Experiences such as domestic violence, abortions, hate crimes, gender equality or anything that had a direct effect personally, showcases your brand values in such a huge way. People don't want to follow anyone who cannot think for themselves or who does not have a strong voice. Your personal brand should have an opinion, otherwise you will quickly fall into the sea of everyone else's.

My personal brand voice stands for women's equality and empowerment. I am a huge advocate of seeing women win in business and in life. I voice this every chance I get. A great deal of the experiences I have had in my career, come off the strength of being an example of a woman that wins.

The next part you want to consider, as far as your personal brand messaging, is to be yourself. If you are struggling to create authentic and valuable content, you do this by literally taking pages from your life. For example, if you are a single mom, your messaging will be those experiences that you encounter every day with balancing children and work. These will be the topics that you blog about, give advice on, share tips about, you name it. You can even create products that mirror your life. For example, I started a kid brand for my son Tyler last year. It started off as a business selling summer treats that my mom used to make for him during the warmer summer days. He enjoyed them so much, we decided other kids would enjoy them too. This turned out to be his very first business. Although he did not have a clue about what was happening at just 2 years old, he made the headlines in the business section of the local newspaper, and received tons of national attention.

Another example of taking a page from your life and turning it into content, would be the time when I turned my first blog series into my first book. Eventually, I shut my blog down and turned it into my first podcast, after noticing that my audience responded better through this channel! (See how your personal brand grows as you grow!).

Years ago, I noticed that I was receiving a ton of questions on how I started my business while working a 9-5. I took those questions and answered them in a 10-day blog post series titled "10 Ways to Start Your Business with 0 Dollars." That series got thousands of hits. When I got pregnant with my son, I decided I had to generate more income. My solution was to write a book. What would I write this book about? Well, about something I already knew and had in the palms of my hands. I took this blog post series, added my personal stories, and published a book. This is how you turn your life into content.

The kind of content you produce is up to you. If you are a writer, turn what you write into blog posts. If you have a captivating voice, turn it into podcast episodes. If you love to be on camera, turn it into YouTube videos. If you love to speak, go and find organizations that can benefit from what you teach or say.

Before we divert from the subject of messaging, I want to point out what I like to call "The K. Michelle Story." K. Michelle came on the scene as a blue haired, wild songstress who appeared to have tremendous talent, but a bad attitude. This was her brand messaging at the time. After becoming a cast member in the early Love & Hip Hop Atlanta days, her brand took a turn. She found herself caught in a lot of controversy over some accusations made about one of her previous relationships. Unfortunately, this then became her brand story. If you followed this story, you probably noticed that although K. Michelle never changed who she was, she changed the direction of her messaging by leaving this particular reality show. She then focused on putting the message she wanted in the front of her audience, which was her music. Since then, she has released record breaking albums and continues to spread her message through her songs. She is still the same wild singing songstress, but changed the narrative of her brand story.

Paying attention to what is happening around you is the best way to create a message that will change your life, and inspire those connected to your brand. I have made this a habit. As I grow and evolve, it translates into my personal brand authentically.

Your Personal Brand Statement

Once you have figured out your personal brand messaging, you will be able to craft your personal brand statement. This statement tells what unique value you offer, who you can help and how you can help them. When you are done reading this section, take a moment and think about your personal brand statement. Remember to make it memorable and catchy. Most importantly, make sure it specifies how you provide solutions. To help you with this, please see a sample personal branding statement formula below:

What are you the best at (value) + **who** do you serve (audience) + **how** do you uniquely serve your audience=
your personal brand statement.

QUICK PERSONAL BRAND STATEMENT FORMULA:

WHAT ARE YOU THE BEST AT (VALUE)
+
WHO DO YOU SERVE (AUDIENCE)
+
HOW DO YOU UNIQUELY SERVE YOUR AUDIENCE
=YOUR PERSONAL BRAND STATEMENT

#BRANDYOULIKEABOSS

CHAPTER THREE

Your Network

Once you tapped into your unique brand message, and know exactly who needs and wants to hear it, you will need a network to keep the message circulating. It is not good enough to have a really intriguing story and great visuals, but do not have a network of people to help spread your message. If you skip this part, your message will not go very far, nor will your personal brand be as effective.

When I refer to your network, I do not mean people within the confinements of your immediate circle of friends and family. Neither am I referring to those you have been Facebook friends with for the last decade. Your network is an extension of you, beyond your four walls and immediate reach in the online space. Over the years, I have learned that having a strong network is an asset to your personal brand. This network becomes your backbone. It becomes a driving force behind everything you stand for. It allows you to be able to execute your goals and touch more lives than your human hands can. Think about it like this: if you are a tree and you have thousands of branches on that tree, that is essentially what your network is going to do for your personal brand. You need this network to keep growing and make the impact you want to make.

We all have heard the statement "It's not what you know, but who you know." I've had my beliefs and doubts about this phrase. For the most part, it is true. This further proves why having a strong network is essential. That's what will bring everything we have discussed in this framework together.

You are who you connect with, and this leaves a lasting impression in the minds of those who will benefit from your personal brand. People pay attention to the people you tag on Facebook, who you show up with to parties and events, and who you sit with in the break room during lunch hour. Although we cannot control every little aspect, we do have control over who we allow in our personal space.

"A strong network is an asset to your personal brand."

#BRANDYOULIKEABOSS

You may be wondering what your network has to do with personal branding, and how they intertwine. Your personal brand is what positions you to make the best first impression when building your network. Imagine you are the new kid on the block, you walk into an environment and are by yourself. You want to make connections, but no one knows who you are. Your first impression is everything that we have discussed in The LMN Approach™ up until now. We talked about your look and messaging. Just like when you are dating and meet someone. If you are a guy and you meet a girl you are interested in, you will make sure you have that fresh cut, white teeth and fresh kicks (because you do know females judge you by those shoes, right? LOL) before that first date. Just as you would try to make the best first impression while dating, the same rules apply when building your network. Why is building a network important? You use your network, credibility and reputation to become the leader in your industry or on your job in corporate America. It is okay to start off teaching to an empty crowd, but at some point, you want those seats to start filling up. You accomplish this by showcasing your credibility consistently.

Before I share with you, how you can start strategically building a network of people who will know, love and trust you, I would like to share a real-life example of the true power of having a network to help you build your personal brand.

It was January 2015, and I had been hired to film on the set of the hit television show Empire, starring Taraji P. Henson and Terrance Howard. It has always been one of my dreams to be able to step foot on a big television set to absorb the energy. I took a leap of faith and applied for an extra role, even though the show was being filmed in

Chicago. It was to my surprise when I received the acceptance email because I was at a very low point in my life. No money, no savings and not sure how I was going to pay my bills that month.

If you know anything about the television industry, you know that extras do not get paid to travel to film. You either need to live in the city or cover your own travel expenses. I knew that this opportunity was not a direct goal to become a big actress or get a lead role. However, I knew it would be a great positioning opportunity to show people I was capable of physically putting myself where I wanted to be. A huge part of my brand messaging was to be known as the girl who made bold moves to motivate others to live their dreams.

I took bold action and knocked out all the excuses of why I could not get to Chicago. To be quite honest, lack of money was my biggest obstacle. Remaining focused, I raised the money in less than 2 weeks. I had heard about crowdfunding, but had never done one before. Desperate, I set up a GoFundMe page without knowing if I had the right setup, copy or if people would even be compelled to donate. All I knew was that I had to share the truth about where I was and what I was trying to do. I waited to see if people would back me. Where did I turn? My network! Now mind you, at this stage I had already lived in multiple cities over the past years so I had built relationships both on and offline with thousands of people around the world. I posted the link to the campaign and people that I didn't know started donating money. People who were leaders in their industries, music execs, film execs, influencers, you name it, were donating. The ones who didn't donate their money, they did their time, by sharing my story and the link for the campaign with people that they knew (their network). I ended up exceeding my financial goal for this opportunity, thanks to my network. It was phenomenal to see how I had invested years building and cultivating the relationships within my network, and now this network was the thing that funded my entire trip to Chicago. This bold move would allow me to better position my personal brand. This trip to Empire for a small role, has now become a major part of my brand story. It has opened many doors for expansion. This further proves that you must have a network who can keep your brand message going.

There are tons of ways you can start strategically building your network. However, I am going to highlight those that will apply to just about any type of personal brand.

Let's talk about a few ways you can start building a network that will contribute to the growth of your personal brand. For starters, you will want to make sure you are sharing (both on and offline) valuable tools, resources and be a "connect" within your industry or niche.

Making your contributions to your network is like making deposits into your 401K. If you keep making deposits, you will have something to withdraw from when the time comes. You cannot withdraw from something you do not contribute to. You want to make sure that you do not just find value in your network when you are on the receiving end. You want to make it a habit to make consistent deposits into those who are in your network. It's something as simple as what types of posts, articles and recommendations you are sharing within your industry. It's good to get in the habit of being "the connect" so that people can trust they can come to you for a reliable referral. Although the referral may not benefit you immediately, by your willingness to give someone else in your network some shine, you become a trusted source which is beneficial in general. As you build your personal brand, you will also want to be more intentional about your shares, retweets and recommendations. It is all a representation of who you are and what you stand for. Ask yourself if what you are sharing is going to be beneficial to your audience or those who you want to position yourself in front of.

MAKING CONTRIBUTIONS TO YOUR AUDIENCE IS LIKE MAKING DEPOSITS INTO YOUR 401K.

Another way I have been able to build a ford tough network is by leveraging social media. Get in the habit of knowing where your audience is hanging out. By investing in other personal brands and other businesses, you become a part of communities that has endless opportunities to network and position yourself. Here's the thing: people love to be recognized. Going back to the Chicago-Empire opportunity, I focused heavily on showing love and recognition for each person that donated. For each person that donated, I created a custom graphic that cost me nothing but time, saying thank you with their individual names. That made them feel good and expressed to my donors, how much I appreciated their support. This simple gesture, resulted in them sharing their appreciation posts, and it brought more awareness to my campaign. These are ways I expanded my personal brand and got my story in the front of people all over. Use social media to grow your network and to show others appreciation and love. Your audience loves when you engage with them by commenting and hopping in their live streams. People pay attention to the people who pay attention to them. This is the key with networking. You must contribute to your industry. In a social media broadcast, people do not know, recognize or remember the person sitting back and not engaging or interacting. They only pay attention to the person whose name they see consistently. While we are on the social media tip, I would like to share another example of how you can not only grow your network, but how you can grow your following on social media.

There is an entrepreneur that I follow. She is a well-known Instagram and brand strategist who shows people how to make money using the Instagram platform. She was also a donor of my Empire campaign a couple of years ago. I did not know her, however she had been following my journey and was compelled to donate. This woman has a phenomenal business and is a leader in her field, making almost seven figures. I have bought many of her e-books, courses and master classes. Basically, anything she created, I bought. She just knows her stuff. She launched an online academy and posted a couple of new courses that I had not owned. I purchased them to see if they would help me to continue growing my Instagram following. When I tell you one of the courses literally changed the game for my Instagram life, it was everything! Excitement of seeing such a quick return on my investment, I immediately took to my Instagram, and told my followers how amazing the course was. I snapped a pic in my stories, tagged her in it and within a matter of five minutes she responded. She was thankful for the feedback so I continued telling her the results I was getting. Within the hour, I received a notification saying that she had tagged me in a post on her Instagram page of over 150k followers! Did I expect this? Absolutely not! I was simply sharing genuine feedback about a product she created where I received real results. She took a screenshot of our conversation and posted it on her page with my name tagged. What do we normally do when someone we are influenced by tags someone in their public posts? We go and click on that person's page, look around and most likely we follow them too! This is exactly what happened within seconds of her tagging me in that post. My follower count grew and so did my engagement that day! Do you see what simple engagement and nourishment of your networking efforts will do for you? After doing it a while, it will eventually become natural and second nature. Again, people pay attention to the people who pay attention to them. Words to live by. Another great way to expand your network that many new brand builders do not consider is guest blogging.

This can also apply to guest vlogging, being a guest on a podcast, Facebook Live, virtual summit you name it. These are strategic ways to expand your brand. What you are doing is being a part of a network that you did not build on your own. When you use these "guest" opportunities to position your personal brand in the front of these new networks, you are sitting at someone else's table. You can now bring some of those people over to your table. This is a great way to be visible and extend your expertise.

Lastly, no matter what industry you are in, make it a habit to devote time each week to meet at least one new person. With the internet and social media, this is probably a low count considering most of us meet at least 10 new people a day online. Meet someone new and exchange information. You will be amazed at how your network will continue to grow with simple introductions.

As you can see, your network is what brings the entire LMN Approach together. You have the look and the messaging which allows you to have a great first impression when building the network that will allow the blood to continue to circulate through your personal brand life.

"Build an empire that will communicate your message to the world."

 #BRANDYOULIKEABOSS

PART TWO

Your Personal Brand Empire

Let's shift gears a bit, and talk about how to consistently communicate your message to the world. The LMN Approach™ gave us the strategy and makeup of your personal brand. Now it's time to build the various channels that will allow you to properly position yourself in the front of those who matter. There are many different moving parts in a personal brand empire, and no you cannot master them all at once. However, when you do, the skies are the limit!

By leveraging the many gateways to delivering your brand story and message, you will find that maximizing platforms, such as podcasting and writing books, will allow you to directly speak to your ideal clients on a platform in which they best receive and retain information. For example, podcasting may be the better option if you have an audience that is busy, always traveling and on the go. This allows for them to access your value in parameters that are in alignment with their lifestyle. Contrary to that, starting your own show on YouTube may be best if you have a younger audience who is better engaged by physically seeing you through videos. The point is, you probably won't use all of the many channels there are to build your personal brand empire. Once you figure out exactly where your audience engages with you the most, you will want to be as visible as possible in those places, providing consistent and high-quality value (no fluff).

Another perk of having a multi-dimensional personal brand empire, are that the chances of missing a prospective customer, client or colleague will be slim. Imagine, you have been looking for some creative ways of gaining new clients for your business, but you only have a couple of YouTube videos posted. You attend a huge conference and meet a couple of very promising clients, but they have no clue how to navigate YouTube. Guess what? Because you did not have any other place to point them to, you could have lost that connection and opportunity to gain a new client. This is what you want to work towards when building your empire.

"Writing books is how you put your money where your mouth is."

 #BRANDYOULIKEABOSS

CHAPTER FOUR

Becoming An Author

Writing books is one of the best ways to build your brand. It is how you "put your money where your mouth is." Becoming an author is becoming more and more common with the easy access to self-publishing platforms such as Createspace, Lightning Source and Nook Press by Barnes & Noble. It has never been easier, so why not add "Author" to your efforts of validation in your industry?

Today, being able to refer someone to your Amazon Author page is more effective than passing them a business card. Why? This says "Hey I do not just have a fancy business card with all of my titles and contact information. Let me show you how I earned these titles and how I can help you!" See. Much more effective!

Writing books that provide solutions and answers for your audience is going to be one of the ways that your brand stands out from others. Books not only allow you to provide solutions and answers, but it is the best platform outside of speaking that allows you to be in control of how your story is told. This is where you will gain trust with your audience. That emotional connection will muster up interest in learning more about you and what you offer. In this case, you are building "the know" and "the trust" factors!

It often amazes me how many people are literally afraid to write a book. Who said you had to make an A+ in high school and college English or have 15 years of experience under your belt? These are not the prerequisites. I often tell people that we are all "experts" in our own right. This means that for as long as you are living and learning each day, rather in life or business, you will always know something more than someone else. The beautiful thing about building an effective personal brand, is that no matter how many other books are on the shelf about the exact topic of your choice, there is no other book on the shelf with your unique story.

One thing that usually puts a halt on a completed manuscript is trying to put your entire life's story and all your years of experience into one book. This is not only absurd, but it is not going to be effective. Here's why: It's 2017 and people just are not reading five and six hundred page books anymore. Especially, if you have not hit "celebrity status" or have starred on the latest season of The Real Housewives of Atlanta. The hard truth is, if you do not fall into these categories, people just don't seem as interested in your life.

I can remember writing my first book; no one knew who I was. I knew I needed a book that was a no brainer to read and easy to digest. The great thing about becoming an author, is you can write as many books as your heart desires. It is a great strategy to keep people coming back for more. You can write books based on each stage of your life or career you are in. For example, my first book was the outcome of what class I had just graduated from (the start your business with 0 funds class). My second book was about my adventure to Chicago and what it took for me to step foot on the set of a hit television show (the dare to live your dreams class). Now here we are at book #3 and you are getting all new experiences, and tested expertise that I have gained over the course of my entire career of building my personal brand. Imagine if I had put all three of these books into one. It would overwhelm us both and you would not have made it past page fifty.

Do not complicate the process of becoming an author. If you must, start off with a simple e-book and build. This will allow people to get to know you, understand your story, mission and values and be ready with card in hand when you release your first 200-page book!

Becoming an author is not only rewarding, but it is almost guaranteed to position you as a thought leader, expert, or influencer within your industry. Besides that perk, it is a great way to position yourself for future opportunities, and did I mention it makes one hell of a business card!

There are typically four different phases of writing a book and becoming an author. These phases are:

1. Before you write the book (prewriting)
2. While you are writing the book
3. Publishing the book
4. Marketing & promoting the book (post-writing)

Now let's talk about what you should be doing before you write and publish your first book. Everyone's process is different, and depending on what your goals are for your personal brand, you will want to adjust the following steps accordingly.

Decide on what topic or life experience you are qualified to discuss. To determine rather or not you are "qualified," take this simple 2 question test.

    a. Have you found a solution in the area or on the topic that you will write about?

    b. Do you know enough about the subject/topic to write an entire book on?

The easiest way to know what type of book to write, is to pay attention to the questions that people ask you all the time. Remember, you can write multiple books for each area of your expertise over time. Do not try to cram all those questions into one book! You will want to make sure that your book inspires, educates and/or enlightens the reader. If you are going to write a book about your life's story, make sure you incorporate it with valuable lessons learned so that the reader has a benefit for reading it.

1. Draft a rough copy of your outline. Include the ideas you have for your book content and put the different ideas into categories that will later turn into chapters.

2. Start writing your chapters. Do not worry about it being grammatically correct at first. Get your ideas on paper.

3. Choose your book title/subtitle.

4. Create your book cover (I highly suggest hiring a professional designer for this!) Your cover will determine in most cases rather or not someone picks up a copy of your book.

5. Once you have finished writing your book content, hire a professional editor to edit for you.

6. Start promoting your book at least 90 days before its release date.

7. Publish your book!

The steps above are just a general step by step guide for writing and self-publishing your book. If you would like more guidance, visit NatashaWeston.com and download the audio on this.

QUICK 2-QUESTION QUALIFICATION ASSESSMENT WHEN DECIDING TO WRITE A BOOK:

A. HAVE YOU FOUND A SOLUTION IN THE AREA OR ON THE TOPIC THAT YOU WILL WRITE ABOUT?

B. DO YOU KNOW ENOUGH ABOUT THE SUBJECT/TOPIC TO WRITE AN ENTIRE BOOK ON?

#BRANDYOULIKEABOSS

From a branding aspect, if you decide to use Amazon's Createspace or any of the free self-publishing platforms, I highly recommend purchasing your own ISBN number. An ISBN stands for International Standard Book Number and this is a 10 or 13- digit number that identifies your book. Basically, this is the "social security number" of your book. ISBN numbers can be purchased individually or in bulk for anywhere between $125 for one, or up to $295 for 10 of them. If you plan to write multiple books over time, you will get a better deal by getting 10 of them at a time. You can purchase your ISBN number at ISBN.org. The reason why you want to avoid the free ISBN number route is because you will have more rights to your book and it looks less amateur. When you are using Createspace's free ISBN number, in the section on your Amazon author's page where it lists the book publisher,

Createspace will be listed there, versus your own name or company name. If you are really on this journey to branding you like a boss, say no to free Createspace ISBN's. Writing books is not only a great way to be seen as a leader, but it is a good way to bring brand awareness.

Have you ever heard of Russell Brunson? Well, Russell is the CEO and Founder of the infamous ClickFunnels. ClickFunnels is a service that many entrepreneurs use in their businesses. At the introduction of this brand, I did not know the person who invented it. As my interest grew in ClickFunnels, I did some research on its benefits for my business. In this research process, I then discovered some videos about its founder. This deterred my interest from the service, to the person who created the service. After watching a ton of his videos, I did not realize that he was the white guy, standing in front of a black chalkboard, in every other advertisement on my Facebook timeline. Ironically, he was the author of a highly raved about book titled "DotCom Secrets." I started to wonder just how many others out there knew about Russell's business (ClickFunnels), but did not know Russell per say. His offer appeared and you would not believe what it was, the chance to get a free copy of his book. Yea, the highly raved about one, in one click! All I had to do was pay for the shipping. I was completely blown away! I had never heard anyone writing a value packed book, and give it away to millions of people. After I finished his first book, I was completely intrigued by his strategies. I opened every single email that came after that book. Not long after reading "DotCom Secrets," his next book dropped called "Expert Secrets," same offer. FREE! With every video I watched and every free book he sent me, I grew more and more in love with Russell's brand. I still have not bought into the ClickFunnels service, however I gained much more value at this stage in my life through his free books.

Get it? Do you see what Russell Brunson is doing to get his books into the hands of his audience? He is making it easy for them to hear his story and get to know him. I am sure in the same way I am sharing his strategy with all of you, many who gets their hands on a free copy of his work will share it with someone they know as well. This my friend, is what you call writing books to build brand awareness.

The possibilities of the many ways you can write and publish books are endless. Becoming an author is one of the few aspects of the personal brand empire that just about anyone can venture into. It is a great way to build credibility, get speaking engagements and it opens the door for invitations on tv and radio shows, podcasts, collaborations, etc. Entrepreneur or not.

"Before someone invites you on their stage, build your own."

 #BRANDYOULIKEABOSS

CHAPTER FIVE

Build Your Own Stage & Speak

Many of you probably do not know, but when I started my speaking career, I did it off a whim and for free. I never looked at free engagements as "Oh I'm not getting paid so I'm not going to give it my all." I pretended that I was getting paid thousands of dollars to speak in the front of thousands of people. I knew that in order for that dream to actually happen in real life, I had to be prepared for it.

Whenever I got asked to attend an event or speak in the early days of my career, I would make sure I had my tripod or my mom there, to catch footage and capture photos and video of me speaking and interacting. I used the footage from free speaking engagements and flipped them into content. I think this is where many miss opportunities. When you are just getting started and on a quest to get others familiar with you and your story, "free speaking gigs" are one of the easiest ways to shine on someone else's platform and reap the benefits. The benefits are content you can use on social media, in your speaking reel, courses, books, YouTube videos, you name it.

Literally, all I did to become a professional speaker, is take all the clips from my free speaking engagements; divvy them up into short 60 second videos and posted them on my YouTube channel. Then I distributed them on my social media networks. It will make your platform look larger than life! It may sound crazy, but these are the exact things you should do to build your brand. When you are building, your focus is sharing life changing content that will enhance people's lives. People will care about who you are and what you have to say. Bottom line. You are going to boost your abilities enough to where others will:

1. **Start to pay attention**
2. **Conform to your expertise**

The end goal of personal branding is to get others to conform to your expertise. Speaking allows you to do this. You can distribute one speaking opportunity into many things.

I did a keynote speech for a financial institution a few months ago. I took an audio recorder along with me to record my speech. Want to know what I did with that recording? I transcribed it and put it in this book. Chapter 9 to be exact on personal branding in the workplace. Why? Well, I have already talked about it before, but many did not have access to the information shared. Now I have turned that one time speaking opportunity into content to put in this book. This one book is going to reach and provide solutions for thousands of people.

One of the questions I get often about speaking is "How do I get people to book me to speak?" My answer is always this: Start speaking now. You cannot expect to wake up one day and decide that you are going to be a speaker. This is a part of the journey of building your personal brand empire. It must be built by becoming a reputable source in your industry or organization. I can almost guarantee you are reading or bought this book from a smartphone, iPad, tablet or other smart device. If you have a smart phone that has a voice recorder on it, start speaking. The voice recorder will become your audience before you have a live audience. Your phone is your speaking practice. I cannot tell you how many times I have walked around my house, turned on my recorder and acted like there were some very important people sitting in the front of me. I spoke as if I was talking to people that didn't know what I knew, and it was my job to teach them. In addition, I would record myself and listened to the playback over and over again to hear the words that I used repetitively and to count the "ums" in my sentences. I did this many, many times, before I ever got booked for anything. Practicing will position you to get the clarity you need on a topic. You want people to know what topics to hire you to speak about or what events to invite you to participate in. Although you can speak on a variety of topics, I advise getting known for one topic first before adding more to your signature speech list.

For example, my very first speaking gig was a meet and greet hosted by a couple of Clemson University students and graduates. Who would imagine right? A college dropout, getting invited to speak to college students and graduates about starting a business? Once again, the power of strong messaging and brand presence. This engagement was not a paid booking, but it made for great practice standing in the front of an audience! They had heard about my first book through social media on how to start a business while working a 9-5. I got clear on a topic," how to start a business with no start up." Therefore, they reached out to me. They knew exactly what they wanted me to come and discuss. Guess who was sitting in the room? A whole lot of college graduates who had degrees, but were curious on how they could multiply their income by starting businesses!

I am now positioned as an expert in this one area. If you can get clear on one topic, you can get clear on many topics. Fast forward to today, I now get hired to speak on multiple topics. I have been able to showcase a level of expertise single handedly and can now provide value to others. When event planners and organizations know you can provide their audiences with value, you are helping them to fulfill their brand's mission. This means you get hired to speak at more events.

Contrary to what you may have heard or have been trained to believe, I do not believe you have to have one hundred paid speaking engagements to prove that you are an expert at something. My first paid speaking opportunity wasn't until my 3rd or 4th time standing in the front of a crowd. Let me address the elephant in the room because I already know you're thinking it. You will have people to tell you never speak for free. At this stage in my career this statement holds truth. However, when you are just getting your feet wet in this arena and working to perfect your signature speech; speaking for free is your training. This phase will help you get rid of speakers' anxiety. Use those free speaking opportunities to get better, add to your portfolio and reel. When it is time to demand payment, you will have a developed a digital resume of past engagements to show. I am pretty sure no one is going to ask if you got paid or how much you got paid to speak.

One last thing I want to mention as you prepare to build your speaking platform. Make sure while you are building that you are getting the logistics of your speaking career prepared. First, you will need to have some idea of what your speaking rates will look like. Trust me, most organizations have a budget allocated for speakers! The worst thing that can happen is to be contacted to speak at an event, and when asked what your speaking fees and requirements are, you start stuttering. This will give off the impression that you are an amateur and have never gotten paid to speak anywhere before.

COMMON SPEAKING CONSIDERATIONS:

-SPEAKER FEE & CONTRACTS

-SPEAKER SHEET

-LIST OF SPEAKING TOPICS

-TRAVEL REQUIREMENTS

-AUDIO/VIDEO ACCOMMODATIONS

snap this!
#BRANDYOULIKEABOSS

Quick story: When I first launched "The Tottie Brand" years ago, one of the first documents I created was a rider. If you are not familiar with a rider, this is a document that is commonly referred to when booking talent for events. A rider basically is a set of requests or demands that an artist, performer, host or speaker sets as criteria for their services or appearances. You may have heard of Beyoncé's extensive rider requirements: VIP dressing rooms maintained at 78 degrees, private bathroom, Pepsi products only, floral arrangements, rose scented candles and on and on and on. Now of course most of us won't have "Queen Bey" styled riders! However, it is good to know exactly what you will require to speak at an event. This could include things like: number of air fare tickets, grade of hotel choice, ground transportation, PowerPoint capabilities, etc. Having a rider early in my career seemed silly, but when I got approached for my first real speaking engagement, I had this information ready to send off. You will want to have materials ready such as a speaker sheet, press kit, professional bio, key topics you speak about, target audiences, speaking contracts. These are all great ways to be in position when the speaking opportunity of your dreams comes.

"Podcasting is the airwave between you and your audience."

#BRANDYOULIKEABOSS

CHAPTER SIX

Launch Your Podcast Like A Pro

Launching a podcast is a great way to showcase your expertise. Podcasting is not new. It has been around for years, but is becoming more mainstream by the day. Entrepreneurs, creatives, brands and even ordinary people with regular lives, are using podcasts as an airwave between themselves and their fans.

You can use a podcast to share your knowledge, wisdom and build a community of your own. By using this medium, you become the voice for your audience, who will look forward to hearing you on a consistent basis. This is a huge advantage for the growth of your personal brand. In most cases, your listeners can consume your content in their comfort zones, making your show a must have in their day to day routines. When you become a part of someone's everyday routine, they feel they know you. This results in the trust needed to have a strong personal brand.

After I started building my speaking platform, I noticed that in between gigs, I had no regular channel to communicate my message, besides social media. I wanted to keep the line of communication open, but could not quite figure out how. Years ago, I launched a blog called Table Talk with Tottie, however because blogging is not something I truly enjoyed doing on a regular basis, I stopped doing it.

One evening, my best friend Regina stopped by. She started telling me about some of the podcasts she listened to every day, either on the way to work or while at work. She is an engineer and spends a great deal of her time at work, but she still had to find a way to consume inspiration and knowledge. She turned to podcasts that she could access right from her smart phone. As our conversation diverted in another direction about general life stuff, she went on to say, "You would do great with a podcast." She expressed how much insight she gained through our conversations and that I should consider putting it on this type of platform.

Without much thought, I restructured my old blog, Table Talk with Tottie, and turned it into my very first podcast.

When starting your podcast, the first step is deciding what type of audience/listeners you want to attract. Next, think about what type of topic(s) you will be talking about. Lastly, decide how frequent you would broadcast.

Deciding on your target audience or who would be listening to your podcast is important. It will help you decide what kinds of topics to focus on. Let's say you are a hair stylist, and your podcast will talk about the truths of the beauty industry for aspiring beauty gurus. You will want to keep up with the latest trends in your industry, and become aware of the discussions many aspiring hair professionals don't get the opportunity to hear.

Starting out, one of my biggest challenges with my podcast was consistency. Unlike other mediums, consistency is the main criteria. It is the only way you will build the momentum and brand awareness you desire. One of the mistakes I made after launching the Table Talk with Tottie podcast, was committing to more than I could handle. I did not take any class on how to tackle the behind the scenes, and technical stuff behind each episode. Therefore, I did not realize how much time and effort was required to get one show posted. Taking a class or having someone who has done this before to show you how, will help you avoid running into the same challenge. When I committed to a new episode every week in my first season, I bit off more than I could chew! I was overwhelmed, but when I changed my posting schedule to bi-weekly, it worked out just fine.

When setting up my podcasting schedule, I like to use the seasonal method. The seasonal method is when you dedicate a certain number of episodes to your podcast, and then go on a hiatus for 2-3 months. You'll find that the length of a season can vary depending on the podcast, however I stick with 12 episodes.

During season one of my podcast, it was a chance for me to introduce myself to my audience. This was the connection channel that let people into my thought process, without having to post directly on social media. My ultimate goal was to build "the know and the like." Other goals were to get familiar with the do's and don'ts of podcasting. This allowed me the chance for trial and error. After I successfully completed my first season of Table Talk with Tottie, I took a hiatus to create new topics and revamp based on the lessons I learned. A hiatus is a break between seasons. Just like our favorite television shows come on for a season, and are replaced with another show during its hiatus. It is the same thing in the podcasting world. How long you choose to take a break is totally up to you.

When I launched the second season of my podcast, my goal was to use it to further position myself as "the connect" within my lane. I brought on some of the leaders in the areas that my listeners were interested in learning from. These guests had powerful brand stories, and provided great value to my podcast. Another goal for my second season was to expand my network. There's a saying that goes something like this: "You can do it all, you just can't do it all alone." This was my exact thought on taking my podcast to the level I dreamed about. I could create hundreds of episodes, and share them with the people who already had a front seat to my brand. However, what good would that do me or my listeners? I had to expand my reach, and I could not do it with just my voice alone. Just as we discussed in the section about networking, when you genuinely shine the light on others, highlight their stories and accomplishments (interviewing others), they are going to be more willing to share. They will share that interview with their network, resulting in your network and podcast growing. Conducting interviews on your podcast is also a great way to continue learning. You can always take away from the person that you are interviewing, which is a plus for life in general.

Another thing I changed in my second season, was the frequency of my show. I went from publishing new episodes bi-weekly to weekly. I did this because I had already learned the process of recording, editing and publishing. I figured out the best ways to get it done efficiently, without spending too much time. A major time saver is bulk recording, editing and scheduling your episodes ahead of time. This will allow you to free up some of your time, so you can keep pushing out consistent content.

Besides a regular podcast show, another great tip for launching a podcast is to create a seasonal show targeted around a specific event, topic or launch. For example, a major part of my marketing plan for this book was a 6-week podcast series, focused on personal branding in the form of informative interviews. I knew that based on the response from my first two seasons of Table Talk with Tottie, I could keep my audience's attention with a more niched show. I had two goals for this series: 1) Provide value in the form of interviews, with individuals who had built successful personal brands, and 2) promote and bring awareness to the book.

The response to this series was almost better than my main podcast. It left my listeners wanting more each week! You can take this same strategy and use it for upcoming projects, launches, events, you name it. It works!

Podcasting is a great way to also practice speaking and building your own platform, especially if you want to become a radio host. There are lots of affordable podcasting platforms you can use to house your episodes, such as Podomatic and Libsyn. Do not get overwhelmed with getting fancy microphones and equipment, because it will stop you from putting content out. I recorded every single episode of my podcasts from the voice recorder on my iPhone 7, and edited it using free software. I literally launched my podcast with less than $10, and created an entire e-course about it!

BULK RECORDING YOUR PODCAST IS A GREAT WAY TO FREE UP YOUR TIME AND STILL PUT OUT CONSISTENT CONTENT.

#BRANDYOULIKEABOSS

In the next chapter, I will show you how I turned this learning experience for my personal brand, into a money-making opportunity! Before we go there, here are the main steps to kick starting your podcast like a pro.

1. Figure out the topics you will discuss, who your target listeners are, and how often you will release a new episode.

2. Figure out what style podcast you will host (solo, interview style, multi-host).

3. Get your cover art design. This is probably the most exciting part, because you will now start to see your podcast come to life! Your cover art should be a representation of your personal brand, personality and what your show is going to be about. I recommend putting your face

on the cover of your first show, so your audience can start associating you with your podcast name.

4. Start promoting your podcast at least 30 days before you publish your first episode. This will build the anticipation within your audience.

5. Record your first episode. Remember, you can use fancy equipment or record directly from your smart phone and send the file to Dropbox or any other file management system for editing.

6. Submit your podcast for approval to the platforms of your choice (iTunes, Google Play, Soundcloud, Stitcher Radio, etc).

These are the basic steps for launching your podcast. However, if you would like more in depth instructions and tips, please visit my website at NatashaWeston.com and purchase the Launch Your Podcast Like A Pro e-course.

"I got a million ways to get it. Choose one."

CHAPTER SEVEN

Monetizing Your Personal Brand

Besides the number one question, "How do I start building my personal brand," monetization is the next most common question. I know you have been waiting to learn how exactly do you get paid for your personal branding efforts. Monetizing your brand is exciting. Everything we have discussed in this book, up until now, has been preparing and positioning you for monetization. If you skipped to this part of the book without reading the previous chapters, go back! That is the foundation you will need in place, before you can start putting dollar signs next to your name. In addition, it is better to have at least one element of your personal brand empire in place and running effectively. This is so you can have something that shows your credibility, and tells brands that you are worthy of working with. Even if you decide you do not necessarily want to work with other brands, you will want to be able to create your own monetization opportunities, which I will share with you later in this chapter.

Finding ways to get paid for being you is important. Today, influencer marketing is on the come up, and fast! According to Traackr.com, influencer marketing can be defined as the process of identifying, researching, engaging and supporting the people who create high-impact conversations about your brand, products or services. Influencer marketing is taking over the traditional ways businesses and corporations advertise their products. The influencer tier is broken down like the following, but can vary depending on who's talking.

Micro influencers are people with smaller followings of 5,000-100,000 followers, and macro influencers fall in the high thousands-millions. Kim Kardashian is a macro influencer. Your favorite YouTuber with 5,000 subscribers would be considered a micro-influencer. Both scenarios have great opportunity to leverage their influence through brand partnerships, or simply creating their own branded products to offer their audiences.

The whole television advertisement era is quickly coming to an end, thanks to social media and regular ordinary people, who have tapped into their personal brands. They can influence millions of people into purchasing products they use daily. For that reason, now is the ideal time to figure out how to monetize your life, and simply be you, and in return get partnerships with brands.

I like to tell people, you need to get in the habit of "linking your life." This means that for just about everything you know, like, wear or for the places you visit, you should be getting paid for it. There should be some type of link, or referral that allows you to get paid a percentage, if not full compensation, for the referrals you make.

The great thing about putting dollar signs behind your personal brand, is that you do not have to be an entrepreneur, business owner or have 1 million subscribers on Instagram to do so. It does helps to have a high number of followers, however most brands look at the engagement you have with those followers instead. You can be working your 9-5 and use your weekend activities or posts on social media, to generate some income on the side. For example, if you are a stay at home mom sharing random photos of your children's most precious moments online, you should be monetizing. Simply start a blog to host these images, with affiliate links that trace back to the toys, clothing or random items seen in your posts. You will be making money without "selling."

"Get in the habit of linking your life."

 #BRANDYOULIKEABOSS

There are all sorts of ways you can make money through your daily life activities. You may have seen me do this with my 3-year old son's personal brand. I created products such as t-shirts and baseball caps, with phrases on them, relevant to his life as a toddler. Whenever I post pictures on his Instagram, I make sure to reference where his fans can purchase the same t-shirts for their toddler boys. You see, everyone has a personal brand, but it is up to you to get creative when it comes to collecting payment. The bottom line is, consumers no longer want to do all their business with corporations, they want to do business with regular ordinary individuals. Consumers trust to purchase products from someone they can relate to, and from someone they can trust the opinions of. As we head full force into this whole influencer marketing era, knowing how to get your audience to trust your day to day opinions and take your referrals, is going to be a huge advantage for your personal brand.

We make most of our purchasing decisions, based off of what other people say about products and services. Therefore, if you incorporate this same concept into your plan to get paid, you will go far. For example, there is a beauty vlogger I am absolutely obsessed with. Although, I am not hardly into makeup, I love the statement t-shirts she wears in almost all her videos or on her Instagram feed. I cannot tell you how many t-shirts I have purchased, simply because she wore them. She influenced my purchasing decision, not once, but many times. This is the power of "linking your life!" Let's say I am following someone on Instagram, and they post a picture sitting out on their patio, wearing some super cute sunglasses. I am going to immediately go and see if she included the name of the store, or a link to where I can learn more about the shades. Even if I do not make the purchase right away, I will eventually go to her link, see if it's within my budget, and the next time I am ready to hit add to cart, I'll keep her recommendation in mind. It is great to get in the habit of retraining your mind to think, okay, if I'm going to tell someone where I got this item, I should see if the company that makes the product or service has some sort of brand ambassadorship or affiliate program. Although most affiliate programs only pay out between 6-10%, it is still money that you can earn.

If you have been connected to me for a while, you probably noticed, I do not promote much on my page, unless it is my product, service, a friend or business colleague's stuff. Making sure that I genuinely believe in and support anything that I promote, is important for keeping my brand values alive. Let me give you an example of how I link my natural love for reading books with monetization. I love collecting books on business, motivation, self-help, branding and social media. This causes me to naturally share my favorite reads with my audience. When I am not voluntarily telling people, they are always asking what books I am reading. I kept getting this question so much, I decided to sign up for Amazon's affiliate program, where I could set up my own Amazon e-store. This allowed me to combine the books in my collection in one space. Every time I post a picture of a book I am reading, you better believe someone will be down in the comment section asking, where they could get the book. Now, I could just automatically tell them to click on the link in my bio (if you are using Instagram) or just put my affiliate link directly in the post (if you are using Facebook or blog post).

There's seriously a million ways to get it...choose one!

Before I tell you the different ways you can monetize your personal brand, let's first do some mindset shifting. To be successful at this, you must first believe people will pay you to be you. If you do not believe it, you will not attract the opportunities you desire. You have to wholeheartedly believe, with hard work and consistency, you are worth it. Confidence seals the deal and pays the bills. If you are walking through the door not confident about what value you can bring to the table, brands see right through it, consumers see right through it, and it will be hard to seal any deals or generate income in your personal brand.

There are three ways you can monetize:

1. **Package your knowledge**
2. **Sell what you use**
3. **Create your own branded products**

Packaging your knowledge is the most common way a personal brand makes money. I am packaging my knowledge as we speak, because I wrote this book. I am telling you what I have learned through experience, trial and error, and researched over the years, as I built my personal brand. I packaged that knowledge, experience and wisdom, and put it into what are now the chapters in this book, and I sold it to you for $19.97 retail, or whatever you paid for it. I wrote this book one time, and it is going to sell for the rest of my lifetime.

Packaging your knowledge does not just have to be in the form of a book. It can be through coaching others. You are exchanging your time for money. You can create things such as mentorship programs, digital products such as e-courses, webinars, e-books, downloadable PDFs or audio. Whatever you have learned or have gotten results in, you can package it up and sell it to help someone else. Create it once and sell it repeatedly!

3 WAYS TO MONETIZE YOUR PERSONAL BRAND:

1. PACKAGE YOUR KNOWLEDGE
2. SELL WHAT YOU USE
3. CREATE YOUR OWN BRANDED PRODUCTS

There are millions of people in search for answers to what you have learned through your experiences. You can literally package any and everything that you know. If you are a baker, you can set up a mentorship program where you show 5 aspiring cake artists how to design cakes, and set up a profitable cake business. You will be exchanging your knowledge and time for money. They will then get value, skills and tools to excel in their business. If you are a makeup artist, you can host an interactive workshop a few times a year, where you show aspiring makeup artists different techniques you have learned. This brings me to the next way to monetize your personal brand.

Sell what you use. This can be anything from face cleanser, makeup, apparel, hair extensions to cameras or lighting equipment. The most common way to sell what you use is through affiliate marketing.

Affiliate marketing is basically when you get paid a commission for promoting another business or person's products and/or services. An example of how I have used affiliate marketing to monetize my brand, is when I packaged my knowledge and created an e-course on podcasting. Remember, we touched on this in the previous chapter on podcasting. Not only do I get paid for the course, but because I was sharing the tools I used for my podcast, I went hunting to see if any of the tools had affiliate programs. Podomatic did, so I signed up for their affiliate program, and I now get paid a commission for every person who uses my affiliate link (which is embedded in the course PDFs!). This is how you think strategically when making referrals we all make naturally throughout the day.

This is how you sell what you use. Amazon has a great affiliate program that allows you to create your own custom online store of products that you use. This program also provides you with a special affiliate link to share when making referrals, or when someone asks you "Where did you get that?" The last, but not least, way you can monetize your personal brand, is by creating your own branded products. Have you ever noticed, whenever I hop on Facebook Live to do a free event, I am wearing one of my own t-shirt designs, or one of my statement mugs somewhere in the background? I'll have you to know, every single time I have done that, my inbox was filled with people asking where I got my t-shirt or complementing my mug. This is why you should create your own branded products. I can send my audience directly to my online shop to purchase these items. The types of branded products you can create are endless. Here are some ideas:

- T-shirts/Apparel
- Hats

- Bags
- Journals/Planners
- Mugs
- Stationary
- Pencils/Pens
- Canvas Art

Besides the three ways I just mentioned to monetize your personal brand, there are some other avenues you can explore as well:

- Network marketing
- Partnerships
- Click for Pay (common for blogs)
- YouTube AdSense
- Live & Virtual Events

Personal brand monetization is happening all around us, both on and offline. It is here, rather you paid attention to it or not. You too can have a piece of this "paid pie" by being more aware and intentional. One last thing to remember, make sure whatever you sell, promote or refer, is something you have used personally and love. Do not put your brand reputation on the line just to make a buck. It is not worth it. If you are a fitness trainer, promoting a makeup collection is not going to make sense. It won't seem realistic to your audience. You want the products and services you use to be something you can honestly stand behind with integrity. The next time you post an outfit picture, or tell someone where you got your waist trainer and water bottle, see if there is a link for it. Make that money honey!

"Your personal brand will sometimes need an internal & external makeover."

#BRANDYOULIKEABOSS

PART THREE

CHAPTER EIGHT

Giving Your
Personal Brand A Facelift

You should by now, understand that personal branding is an ongoing process of self-development. It is also largely about telling the story that will resonate with your audience. This means, if you are finding yourself in transition from being well known for one thing, and now you're on to the next, maybe you consider re-branding. Even if you possibly got caught with a bad rap sheet for something that left an ugly stain on your brand, don't fret, this is what rebranding is for!

This strange transition will become familiar as you grow within the comforts of your personal brand. People may be confused for a bit, but remember, you have the power to narrate the story. At some point (and sometimes often), your personal

163

brand will need both an internal and external makeover. As we grow and evolve, so will our brands. It is inevitable. Any brand that does not get a frequent makeover is not going to make its greatest impact. It is like fresh produce in the grocery store. If the store does not sell out of or get rid of expired goods, no one will buy it. It starts changing colors and is not very inviting. The same happens when we are not constantly looking for ways to re-position, and brush up our brand story, positioning and presentation.

ASK YOURSELF (REPUTATION CHECK):

A. WILL THIS THING, ACTION OR STATEMENT BUILD TRUST AMONGST MYSELF, MY BRAND AND MY AUDIENCE?

B. WILL MY IDEAL CUSTOMER, CLIENT OR AUDIENCE LOVE WHAT I AM ABOUT TO POST, SAY OR HOW I AM ABOUT TO ACT?

C. WILL MY IDEAL CUSTOMER, CLIENT OR AUDIENCE TRUST ME AFTER I MAKE THIS STATEMENT OR TAKE THIS ACTION?

#BRANDYOULIKEABOSS

The first step when revamping your personal brand is to "check your reputation at the door." Taking inventory and doing an audit of the current state of your brand is important. You need to be real about where you stand now, so you understand what you need to tweak moving forward. Are people inspired by you? Do people get negative vibes from your brand? What exactly is your reputation right now? It is important to ask ourselves these questions, not only in the early stages of brand building, but frequently along the journey. The best way to do this type of assessment is to ask those who you interact with. You can survey your audience, family and friends or you can do a quick exercise that I love doing. All you do is hop on Facebook and make a status asking: "What are 3 words that you think of when you hear my name?" You'll quickly see some of the similarities in responses. This will give you an idea of what people are saying about you when you are not in the room. You can then adjust accordingly.

Next, understand that when giving your personal brand a makeover, it is important to identify your new goals and make sure the connection between you and your audience is still there. When "life happens," it is easier to just "get through" first and leave everything else for when things get better. Here's the thing: you build the strongest connection within your brand when people feel they are on the journey with you.

Think about the last time your friend put you on hold on the telephone and didn't click back over until minutes later. Didn't like it huh?

If you struggle with figuring out how to reposition your message, share what I like to call your "right now story." Your right now story can be a lesson learned from a recent life experience, or if you're feeling bold, tell your audience what challenges you are facing at this very moment. The point is, by keeping your followers and/or audience current with the happenings in your life, they will feel like you trust them and in exchange they will trust you. It's almost like making up after a break up with your significant other. By telling your audience the scope of your transition, you should focus on the lessons and solutions that came as a result.

The next step when giving your brand a makeover is to simply reintroduce yourself. If you have been in the slumps about your brand not reaching the masses, do not fret. A simple reintroduction is all you need to get your audience excited again. A great way to do this is to share your newest project with them. If your goal is to change the story from your past, unveiling something new within your brand is a good way to showcase your current skills and mission.

Lastly, make sure your visual brand is in alignment with your new brand goals. The whole purpose of a makeover is to show off your new look right? Therefore, getting a new and exciting look is going to really put some spunk in your branding. Hire a graphic designer that can bring your updated story to life, and share them with your audience!

These are some basic ways to give your personal brand a makeover, however I want to touch on a couple of things that tend to tarnish a lot of personal brand reputations. These two things are social media and the internet. Always be mindful of what you put out there. Share carefully, and ask yourself is it going to make or break the image we have talked about all throughout this book. Branding is all about building a reputation, and managing the perceptions that the world has of you. I would like to provide you with a tip for checking your personal brand reputation as you continue to grow and expand. This will serve as the "reality check" we all need.

Ask yourself if what you are doing, saying or how you are acting is an asset or liability to your personal brand. Let's take it a little deeper. Ask yourself:

a. Will this thing, action or statement build trust amongst myself, my brand and my audience?

b. Will my ideal customer, client or audience LOVE what I am about to post, say or how I am about to act?

c. Will my ideal customer, client or audience TRUST me after I make this statement or take this action?

For example, when you make the commitment to build your personal brand and are in it not just for the money, but to make an impact in people's lives, you are going to have to suck some things up. You will have to make some hard decisions, because we are human and there are going to be times where you will want to lash out and react negatively. As a committed brand builder, remember that you are in control of the story that is being told about you, rather you are having a bad day or not. By asking yourself these series of questions, you will be able to determine rather or not something is going to result in being an asset or liability for your brand.

"Your personal brand is the language you speak in the workplace."

 #BRANDYOULIKEABOSS

CHAPTER NINE

Personal Branding in the Workplace

Just as the subject of personal branding has become a leader in conversation over the past several years, so has its popularity in the workplace. Understanding your worth and value at your place of employment, is just as important as it is, if you are an entrepreneur or business owner. Knowing how to showcase your unique value at work, is going to position you for career advancement opportunities within your organization. On the flip side, your audience in the workplace will be your supervisors and coworkers. Tapping into the power of your personal brand in the workplace is what is going to differentiate you from the rest. Some in the workplace, are striving for similar goals. Knowing how to showcase your personal brand today is going to give you the leadership position of your dreams tomorrow.

Believe it or not, it was not too long ago I was still working in Corporate America. Prior to venturing into the world of entrepreneurship full time, I was a mortgage documents clerk and a deposit operations specialist at two different financial institutions in South Carolina. Although both jobs were in the same industry, I had two completely different experiences, as far as the growth I experienced. I was about 25 years old in my first position and was hired as a temp. There were no permanent long-term assignments or promises to get hired on full time with benefits. I was the youngest of all my coworkers. From what I could tell, I was just another "temp" passing through. The pay was a dollar more than minimum wage and my day-to-day tasks were boringly repetitive. Despite the nature of the job description, I liked my job overall and most of the people I worked with. The only problem I struggled with thinking is, do I give this unpromising position 100% or do I just "get by" until my temporary assignment ends. After being there for a few months, I learned that in the banking industry, many of the full-time permanent employees started off in the same position, a temp. They had to show they added extreme value to the company before they were offered benefits and a raise. I set out to do the best at my job and constantly learn more so I could prove I deserved advancement. This was my first time tapping into my personal brand, without even knowing it.

Many in the workplace, go to work each day, clock in and do what they are told to do. However, not often do they extend themselves and do some of the things they are passionate about. This is where I started to tap into my unique value. I started paying attention to the qualities that my supervisors and coworkers pointed out to me all the time. They liked that I was young and eager to learn. They admired my ability to use the computers and machines to do our work assignments. With that information, I too started to notice that I became the "go to" person whenever someone had technical issues with their computers, or needed help finishing a task with tight deadlines. I became known for those things. Being fast, efficient and technically savvy became my personal brand on the job. This was my unique value. These were the things that set me apart from others in my organization. Your personal brand is the language you speak in the workplace. In order for you and the company to grow, you must understand your unique position. Earlier this year, I was invited to deliver a keynote speech for TD Bank. I was quite impressed to learn they wanted me to come and teach their employees about how to build their personal brands at the organization. This came as quite a surprise. I had never known of any large corporations to see the importance of personal branding. Typically, they offer their employees customer service trainings. This is evidence that some of the world's largest corporations are looking for the best of the best to work in their organizations, and to provide extreme value to them. They are seeking out those who have strong and effective personal brands. This is what equates to big business and ultimately big money.

When you tap into your personal brand and contribute the best to your organization that organization gains more customers and brings in more revenue. What does that mean for you as the employee? Raises and promotions.

I typically enjoy educating those in the workforce about personal branding. It is going to become the biggest strategy of your career. This is a topic that rarely trickles down to employees of corporations. Personal development is mostly discussed amongst the leaders of the organization. You may have the best qualities and skills, but if you do not take the time to develop them, you are truly doing yourself and organization a huge disservice. You may still be wondering how your personal brand factors into your current position. Here is a quick diagram that can best demonstrate this:

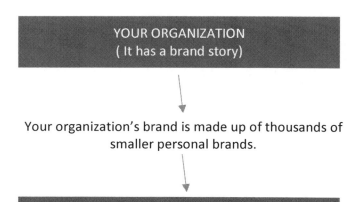

Your job is to manage the impression others have of you. To manage this impression, you must first break down what your personal brand consists of in the workplace. Let's divert back to the original definition of personal branding. It is:

What you say: What conversations are you having (informative, encouraging, gossip?)

What you do: Are you being nice to others? Are you going above and beyond for the team, or are you just doing your part and nothing more?

How you respond: How do you respond to coming back to work, after a not so enjoyable weekend? Do you take it out on your co-workers or do you express what happened, so you can still remain pleasant to work with?

How you interact: What is your body language saying? How are you working the room? Are you giving eye contact and shaking hands, or are you sitting in the back during the team meetings?

Here's the thing: You are going to have days where you may not "feel like" keeping your personal brand in mind. You are entitled to those bad days, but remember it is important to try your best not to show these bad days at work. Your decision not to, could be resting upon your organization gaining a new customer, or you are getting recommended for the position that just opened. You are an intricate part of the way your organization performs each and every day.

Next, I want to point out some ways you can begin to develop your personal brand in the workplace. The first step is to know where you stand right now. Are you in the position that you really want? Are you truly working your skills? Are you constantly learning more so you can advance those skill sets? Ask yourself The Big Question. What do you want to be known for at your organization? This is how you evaluate if you are walking in the power of your personal brand. The next level of this evaluation is to know what is the current perception others in your organization have of you. Pay attention to the comments and statements made about and to you and adjust as necessary.

- Are you known as the self-starter?
- Are you known for gossiping about your co-workers at every turn?
- Are you identified as easy to work with?

The next step in building your personal brand in the workplace is to simply have a plan. This plan will outline what action steps you need to take to better position yourself to reach your goals. You will want to ask yourself the following questions:

- Do I need another degree?
- Do I need more experience?
- Should I seek guidance from someone who is in the position that I want?

The last step to building a personal brand that shines in the workplace, is to show up and act the part. Acting the part is exactly how you set yourself apart. Although you may not have the position or title you want, show up to work each day with a winning attitude. Your attitude and determination to go above and beyond is what is going to get you to the top of that ladder.

CONCLUSION

You are officially a BRAND BOSS!

Pat yourself on the back, however the real work begins now. I have provided you with the framework, tools and strategy that you will need to build an authentic personal brand; now it is up to you to do the work!

What I have shared with you in these pages has been proven to work in my brand and for the hundreds of individuals who I have advised and consulted over the years. It is time to break the barriers and design the life that you desire, starting with the real you.

Congratulations on taking the first step in investing in this book. Personal branding and personal development go hand and hand, therefore I vowed to pour years upon years of personal experience into this book. I encourage you to continue being you, build a brand around who you are authentically and watch the world begin to know, LOVE & trust you!

GLOSSARY

Affiliate marketing: a marketing arrangement by which an online retailer pays a commission to an external website or person for traffic or sales generated from its referrals

Affiliate program: an automated marketing program that involves two or more parties that work in conjunction to provide a certain level of benefit to each other

Audience: a target market or select group of potential or current consumers in which a business or individual aims its marketing and advertising strategies towards to sell a product or service

Authenticity: the quality of being genuine or real

Backdrop: the scene or scenery that is in the background of photographs

Blog series: a sequence of blog posts on a particular topic or subject

Brand elements: a representation of tangible elements that create a visual, auditory, and olfactory brand identity. Includes: logo, slogan, packaging, colors, fonts)

Brand partnership: also referred to as co-branding; a marketing partnership between at least two different brands of goods or services

Brand story: a cohesive narrative that encompasses the facts and feelings that are created by your brand

Brand Strategist: works to ensure a consistent and effective brand message; often forward-thinkers who anticipate future trends and success of a product or service

Brand style guide: the primary visual DNA of your brand; a document that describes, defines and presents examples of what your brand looks like in various visual media such as print, internet and broadcast

Brand values: the emotional currency of your life; the core principles that give meaning to your life and are defined as a set of standards that determine your attitudes, choices and actions

Brand voice: your brand's opinion

Collaboration: the action of working with someone to produce or create something

Consistency: the achievement of a level or performance that does not vary greatly in quality over time

Content: relevant and valuable information used to attract, acquire and engage a clearly defined and understood audience

Dropbox: is a place to store photos, docs, videos and other files

Engagement: active involvement and responses within an audience

Expertise: expert skill or knowledge in a particular field

Direct Message (DM): a messaging function on social platforms that allow you to send private messages to specific users

Facebook Live: Facebook's broadcasting stream that allows you to interact with viewers in real time

Framework: a structured outline used to achieve a particular goal

Headshot: a common type of photograph of a person's face or head and shoulders

Hiatus: a pause or gap in a sequence, series or process

HTML color code: HTML tags for setting background and font colors

Influencer marketing: a form of marketing that focuses on using key leaders to drive a brand's message to the larger market

Influencer: the individual whose effect on the purchase decision is in some way significant or authoritative

ISBN: also known as an International Standard Book Number; a unique numeric commercial book identifier assigned to each edition and variation of a book

Keynote speech: the main speech given at a gathering or event that sets the underlying tone and summarizes the core message

Leverage: use something to maximum advantage

Lifestyle photo: a kind of photography that mainly aims to capture portraits/people in situations, real life events or milestones in artistic manner and the art of the everyday

Micro influencer: everyday consumers who have 500-5,000 highly engaged followers around relevant topics

Monetizing: convert into or express in the form of currency

Network: a group or system of interconnected people

Niche: denoting or relating to products, services or interests that appeal to a specialized section of a population

Personal brand empire: a collection of avenues in which an individual can communicate their brand message; examples are podcasting and writing books

Personal brand statement: 1-2 sentences answering what you are best at, who you serve and how you do it uniquely; it sums up your unique promise of value

Personal branding: the practice of people marketing themselves and their careers as brands; the ongoing process of establishing a prescribed image or impression in the mind of others about an individual, group or organization

Podcasting: the practice of using the Internet to make digital recordings of broadcasts available for downloading to a computer or mobile device

Press kit: a package of promotional material provided to members of the press to brief them about a product, service, project or candidate

Reputation: the beliefs or opinions that are generally held about someone or something

Retweet: repost or forward of a post on Twitter

Rider: a set of requests or demands that an individual (usually an artist or speaker) sets as criteria for an appearance or performance

Self-publishing: to publish a piece of work independently at one's own expense

Speaker sheet: a document that provides an overview of a speaker and their current speaking topics

Speaking engagement: a promise or agreement where a speaker is scheduled to speak at a specific event

Styled photo: a photograph taken in a controlled environment that includes props and different objects that stage a scenery

The BIG Question: the main question that pieces the contents of a personal brand together

The LMN Approach™: Natasha's 3-part framework that is the canvas in which a personal brand is built

NATASHA WESTON

RESOURCES

Tools:

- Canva
- Color-Hex.com
- ISBN.org
- Createspace
- Lightning Source
- Nook Press by Barnes & Noble
- Photoshop
- ClickFunnels
- Dropbox
- Podomatic
- Libsyn
- Amazon Associates (Affiliate Program)

Books Referenced:

- DotCom Secrets- Russell Brunson
- Expert Secrets- Russell Brunson

Credits

- Traackr.com
- Snapchat logo
- Twitter logo

- "A Dream"- Jay Z (lyrics from The Blueprint 2: The Gift & The Curse)
- "I Got A Million"- Jay Z (lyrics from The Blueprint 3)

About the Author

Natasha 'Tottie' Weston is a native of Mount Pleasant, SC and currently resides in Summerville, SC. She is an entrepreneur and the Chief Brand Strategist at The Tottie Brand. She has over five years of experience showing her audience how to acknowledge, build and cultivate their personal brands to become better leaders for tomorrow.

Natasha is a sought after motivational speaker for entrepreneurs and professionals who want to learn her easy to understand approach on personal development and business.

She is an official member of the Forbes Coaches Council, an invite only organization for successful business and career coaches. She has also been recognized by The White House for her work in gender equality at the United State of Women Summit in Washington, DC. As of today, she has been featured by an array of businesses, publications and blogs such as Sheen Magazine, Today's Black Woman and Market America.

Natasha is also the author of two other books titled, *10 Effective Ways to Start Your Business with 0 Dollars* and *Dare to Live Your Dreams.*

Learn more about Natasha by visiting NatashaWeston.com and connect with her across social media platforms @OfficialTottie!

Acknowledgments

At the third book, I guess you can imagine a lot has changed. One of those things, the length of my acknowledgement page in my books LOL. Thank you God for giving me this amazing gift. You so lit.

Tyler, thank you for being mama's side kick and daily motivation!

Mama, we made it! You are the best example of what it means to never give up and we are one step closer to seeing those abundance of blessings here on earth. I won't stop until I can give you the world. You deserve it (and that's an understatement).

Daddy, you already know. You believed in me when I didn't think anyone else did. For that, I will give you retirement sooner than you think.

To my little sister Trish: Thank you for being my best friend when I need you most. I'm still waiting for you to move in so I can have a full-time photographer!

To my amazing team and all of my supporters, family & friends: thank you for rooting for me! You are the real MVP.

NOTES

NATASHA WESTON

BRAND YOU LIKE A BOSS

NATASHA WESTON

BRAND YOU LIKE A BOSS

_____

_____

_____

_____

_____

_____

_____

_____

_____

_____

_____

_____

_____

_____

NATASHA WESTON

_____

_____

_____

_____

_____

_____

_____

_____

_____

_____

_____

_____

NATASHA WESTON

BRAND YOU LIKE A BOSS

_____

_____

_____

_____

_____

_____

_____

_____

_____

_____

_____

_____

_____

NATASHA WESTON

_____

_____

_____

_____

_____

_____

_____

_____

_____

_____

_____

_____

_____

_____

_____

_____

_____

_____

_____

_____

_____

_____

_____

_____

_____

_____

_____

NATASHA WESTON

BRAND YOU LIKE A BOSS

_____

_____

_____

_____

_____

_____

_____

_____

_____

_____

_____

_____

_____

NATASHA WESTON

BRAND YOU LIKE A BOSS

_____

_____

_____

_____

_____

_____

_____

_____

_____

_____

_____

_____

_____

_____

NATASHA WESTON

BRAND YOU LIKE A BOSS

_____

_____

_____

_____

_____

_____

_____

_____

_____

_____

_____

_____

NATASHA WESTON

_____

_____

_____

_____

_____

_____

_____

_____

_____

_____

_____

_____

_____

_____

_____

_____

_____

_____

_____

_____

_____

_____

_____

_____

_____

_____

BRAND YOU LIKE A BOSS

_____

_____

_____

_____

_____

_____

_____

_____

_____

_____

_____

_____

_____

_____

NATASHA WESTON

BRAND YOU LIKE A BOSS

_____

_____

_____

_____

_____

_____

_____

_____

_____

_____

_____

_____

_____

_____

NATASHA WESTON